THE BELLY STiCKER BOOK

duopress

Concept: duopress labs
Art Direction: Violet Lemay
Illustrations: Margie and Jimbo
Design: Beatriz Juárez
Production: Doug Wolff

Cover Photo: Paul Hakimata © 123RF.com

Warning: Only use stickers on fabrics like cotton, wool and polyester.
Not recommended for use on leather or baby skin.
Tested per CPSIA standards.

Scan this
QR code
to explore
more titles
from duopress

To order: hello@duopressbooks.com
Copyright © 2018 by Duo Press, LLC
All rights reserved. First Edition
Manufactured in China
10 9 8 7 6 5 4 3 2 1
Nontoxic
Duopress, LLC
8 Market Place, Suite 300
Baltimore, MD 21202
Distributed by Workman Publishing Company, Inc. / www.workman.com
Published simultaneously in Canada by Thomas Allen & Son Limited.

www.duopressbooks.com

Congratulations! You have a new baby!

Your baby will grow and change at an amazing speed, and every month will bring new and exciting developments. So many, in fact, that you may wonder how you are going to remember all the wonderful events that are coming your way.

Well, this book will help you celebrate your baby's milestones, holidays, month-to-month anniversaries, and other wonderful moments and let you share them with your friends and family on social media or simply create a wonderful photographic memory of your first year together.

From the first smile to your first Mother's Day together, the first birthday to a very bad hair day, use these stickers to help create an entire year of memories.

Just peel, stick, and click.

Use the hashtags

#bellystickers and #bellystickerbook

for extra sharing!

duopress

48 DIFFERENT WAYS TO CELEBRATE!

PAGES 6-31

Make the *FIRST YEAR* of your baby's life a year full of fun.

From month one to your baby's first birthday!

PAGES 32-55

You won't want to miss the celebration. Use these stickers to commemorate a full year of holidays, from the *NEW YEAR* to *CHRISTMAS* and *HANUKKAH*.

PAGES 56-75

Use these stickers to mark random, fun events, from a bad hair day to a day full of LOLs.

Stickers to celebrate month by month!

PAGES 76-104

FIRST SMILE? FIRST VACATION?
Your baby will accomplish tons of milestones in his or her first year. Snap a photo after the first bath or during a great crawl.

CONGRATS!

Let's celebrate your

first month!

Another month.

By now you know
a trick
OR

TWO!

HURRAY!
HURRAY!
HURRAY!
You are three months old!

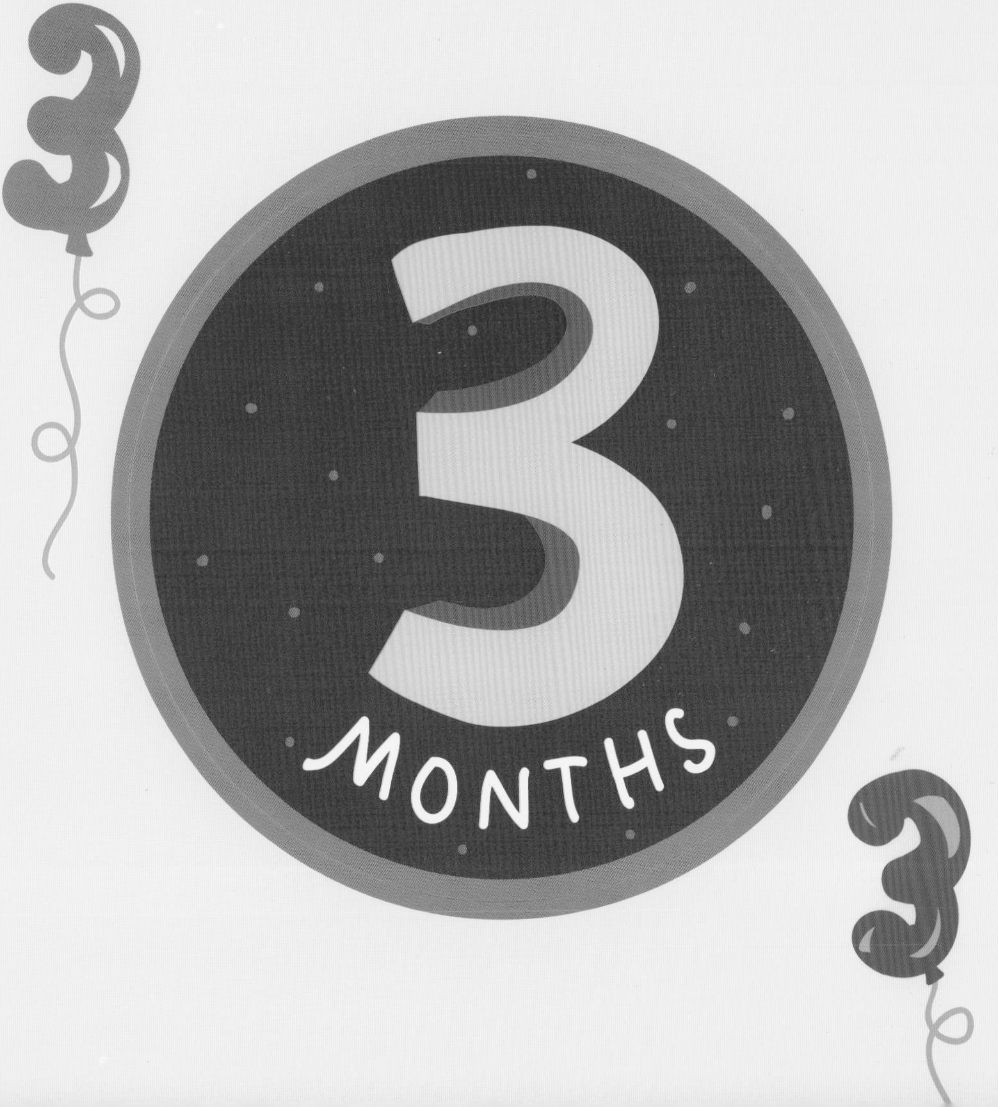
3
MONTHS

It's PARTY Time!

Congratulations
Félicitations
Complimenti
Parabéns
Felicidades
축하해요
ユバ ㄥㄲㄲ
おめでとうございます
祝賀

You're halfway
through your

FIRST
YEAR!

Congrats!

6
MONTHS

You are
SEVEN
times
♥ CUTER ♥
today!

Hip Hip
hooray!
Hip Hip
hooray!
Hip Hip
hooray!

We are all on

CLOUD NINE

for you!

FIESTA
time!

You are almost
one year
old!
YIPPEE!

Happy 1st BIRTHDAY!!

happy 1st Birthday!!

10...9...8...
7...6...5...4...
3...2...1

Bee
♥ my ♥
Valentine.

Connect the dots for good luck!

36

Happy Easter!

happy EARTH Day

MOM

madre

Okaasan

Mére

Mamá

Ahm

Mat'

42

nana

DAD

PAI

Pa

Papá

Padré

Appa

Today is our country's BIRTHDAY.

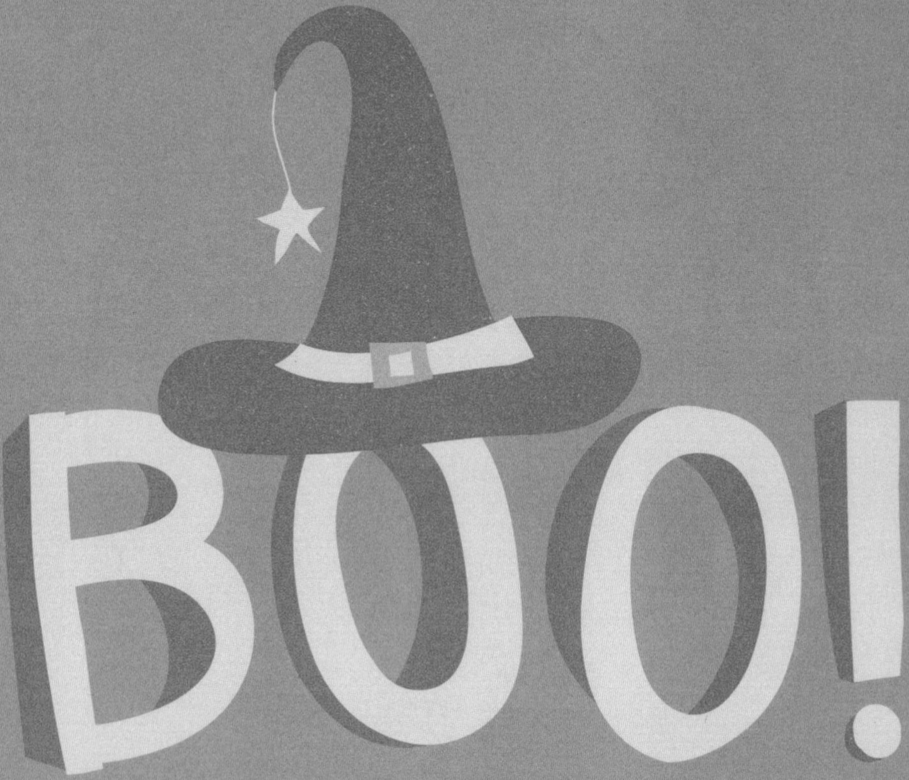
BOO!

Happy Hanukkah

MY FIRST
Hanukkah

Peace,
Happiness,
Health,
and
Fun!

You make me

LOL

all the time!

I don't know much.

It's been a long week:
EAT. SLEEP. POOP. REPEAT.

PARTY

at my

CRIB

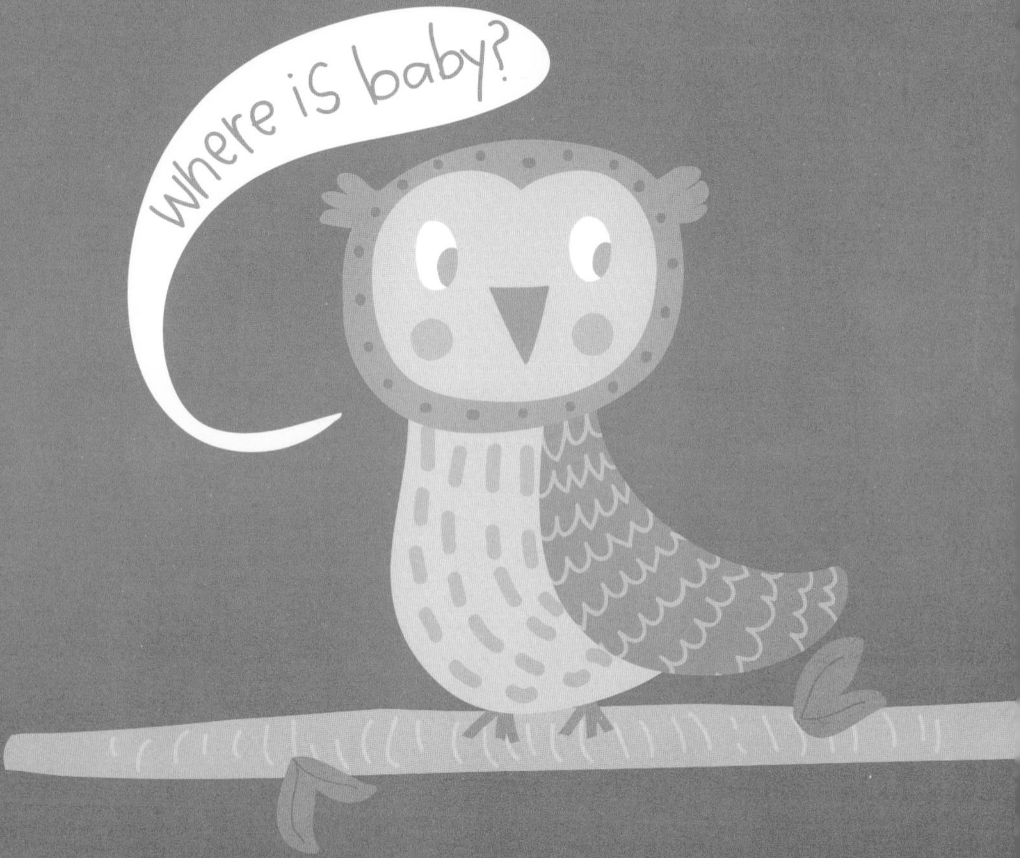
Where is baby?

I'm a bookworm in training!

I RECOMMEND this BOOK

GOT PIZZA?

yum

I WANT PIZZA

mmm!

Where are my TEETh?

TO: EVERYONE

FROM: BABY

SUBJECT: OUT OF OFFICE

I AM AWAY FROM MY CRIB WITH LIMITED ACCESS TO EMAIL.

—BABY

WHOA!

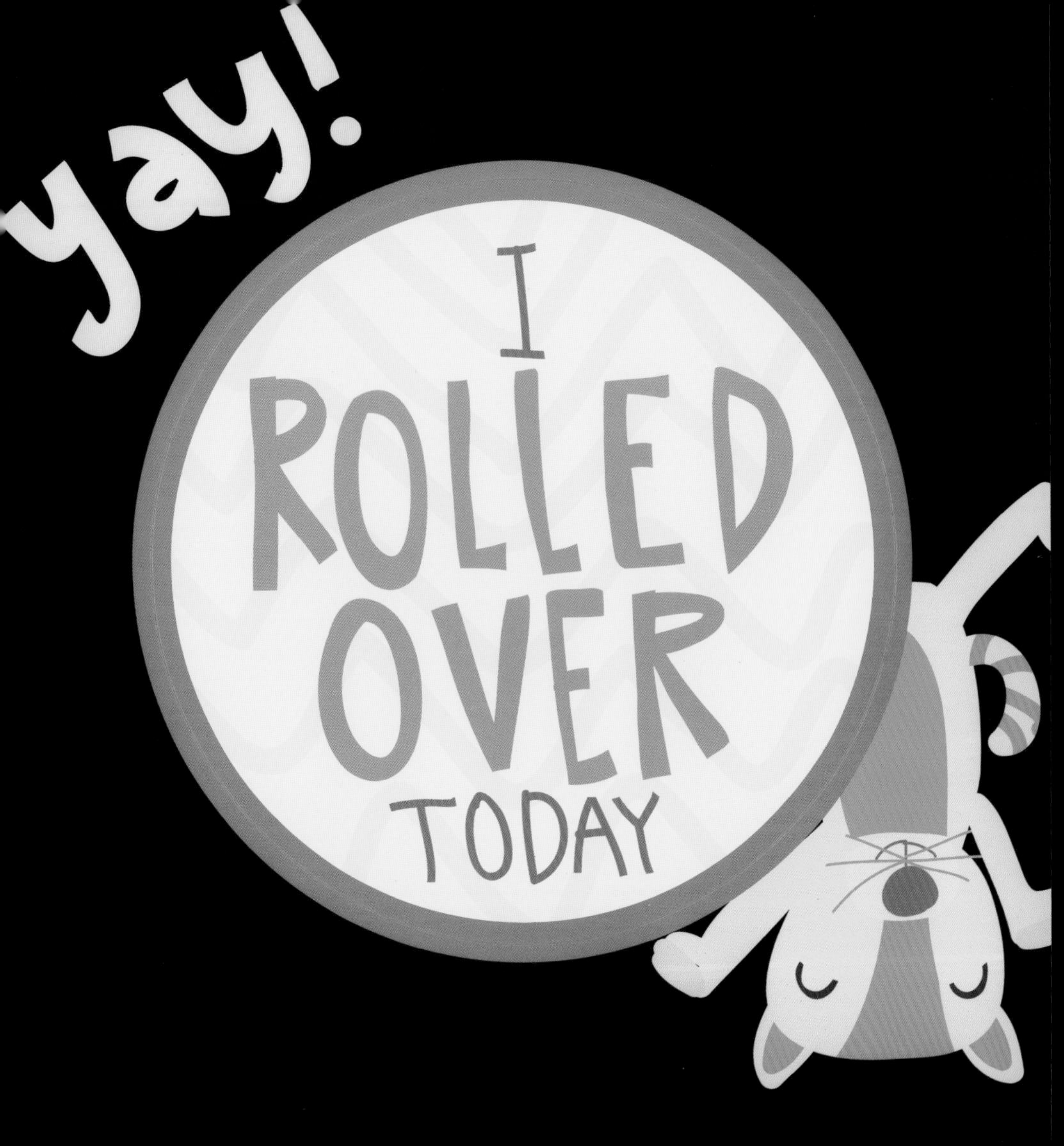
yay!
I ROLLED OVER TODAY

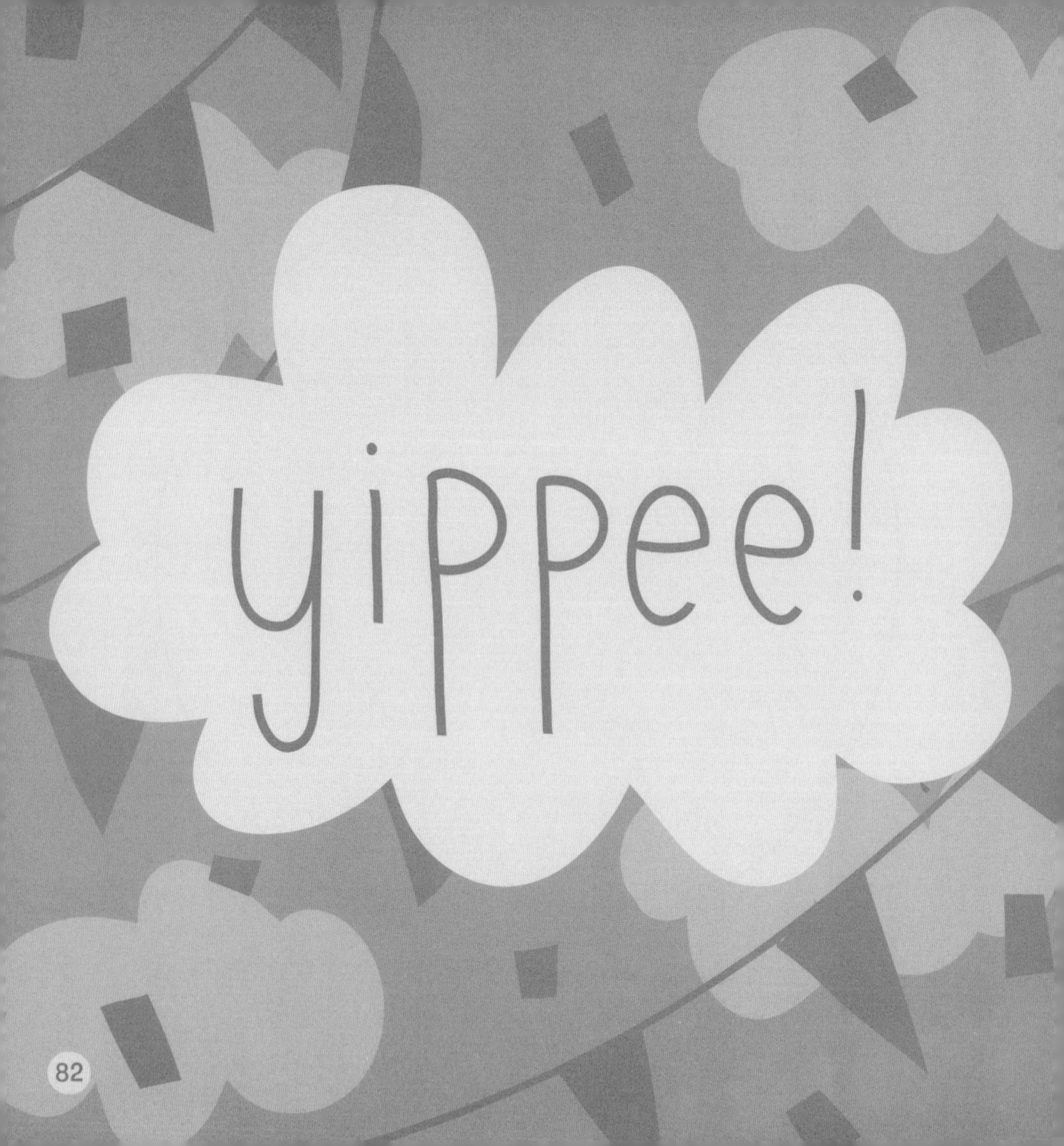
yippee!

mmmm...

my first SOLID food

yum!!!

YAY baby!

I crawled today

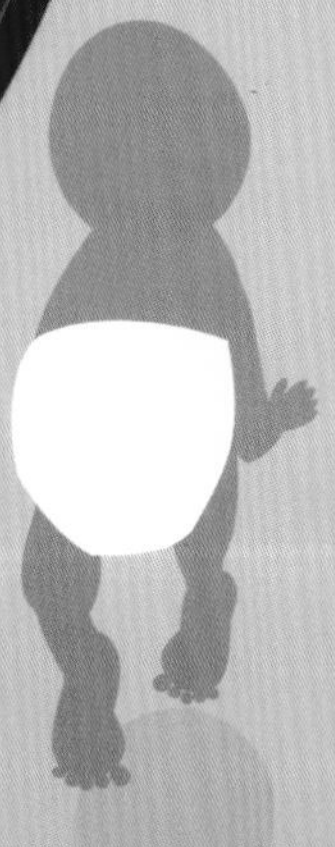

THINGS LOOK DIFFERENT FROM UP HERE!

92

ONE SMALL STEP FOR BABY, ONE GIANT LEAP FOR OUR FAMILY.

I owe my fame
to my
PHOTOGRAPHER

I RULE
social
media

Knock, knock.
Who's there?
Orange.
Orange who?
Orange you happy
to see me?

HA!   HA!

HA!   HA!

my first

LAUGH

HA!

HA!

HA!

HA!

adiós

adieu

ADDIO

adeus

aloha

zàijiàn

Use the hashtags

#bellystickers and

#bellystickerbook

for extra sharing!